I0017427

COPYRIGHT © 2022 LARY ANTHO

Table of Contents

iOS 16 – SUPER GUIDE

OVERVIEW

In June 2022, Apple gave a sneak look at iOS 16, the most current cycle of the iPhone's working framework. iOS 16 has another Lock Screen that can be tweaked, as well as extra sharing, correspondence, and knowledge capacities.

In iOS 16, the Lock Screen has been totally updated, with new elements. The new Lock Screen might be totally tweaked. The iCloud Shared Photograph Library permits relatives to share an assortment of pictures. Messages have likewise gotten significant changes, including the capacity to alter and eliminate messages. Mail, Live Text, and Visual Turn Upward have likewise been moved along.

iCloud Shared Photograph Library permits you to impart a photograph assortment to relatives. Messages have additionally gotten significant overhauls, including the choice to change or erase messages as well as banner them as uninitiated. There are likewise different improvements to Mail, Live Text, and Visual Gaze Upward.

Apple Pay Later permits you to pay for Apple Pay merchandise in portions, and the Wallet application likewise incorporates extra devices for following conveyance and exchanges, checking with advanced ID, and sharing urgent computerized cards.

iOS 16 is viable with iPhone 8 and resulting models. An engineer beta rendition of the update is by and by open, and a public beta will be delivered in July. iOS 16 will be officially delivered in the fall.

Instructions to DOWNLOAD AND Introduce IOS 16

iOS 16 is presently under beta testing to give Apple time to clean the overhaul and settle any defects, as well as to give engineers time to fabricate their applications. iOS 16 is right now open to designers with viable gadgets, with a public beta coming in July.

The redesign isn't supposed to be broadly open until not long from now. At the point when iOS 16 is authoritatively sent off in the fall, any qualified iPhone will actually want to refresh to it by means of the Product Update segment of the Settings application.

CURRENT VERSION

One beta version of iOS 16 has been distributed to developers by Apple. The first public beta version has yet to be released.

CUSTOMIZABLE LOCK SCREENS

The iPhone's Lock Screen has been redone in iOS 16, permitting clients to make various customized Lock Screens and basically move between them with a swipe.

Clients might pick a new multifaceted impact for backdrops that puts the subject before the clock, as well as change the presence of the date and type with an assortment of type styles and variety choices.

Another display highlights backdrops for live climate, pictures of the Earth, moon, and nearby planet group, emojis, and that's just the beginning, as well as suggestions for clients to fabricate customized Lock Screens.

Gadgets motivated by Apple Watch intricacies have been added to the Lock Screen, empowering fast admittance to data like as impending schedule occasions, climate, battery levels, alerts, time regions, Action ring progress, and that's just the beginning.

NOTIFICATIONS AND LIVE ACTIVITIES

In iOS 16, warnings have been acclimated to move up from the lower part of the screen, guaranteeing that clients can see their modified Lock Screen obviously.

From the Lock Screen, users may keep track of activities that are happening in real-time, such as a sports event, workout, ride-share, or food delivery order.

IMPROVED FOCUS MODES

Last year, iOS 15 presented center modes, which have now been improved and cleaned in iOS 16, iPadOS 16, watchOS 9, and macOS Ventura. Each Center mode currently has an associated Lock Screen, notwithstanding the new adjustable Lock Screen in iOS 16. Notwithstanding the recently referenced techniques for initiating a Center mode, for example, through Control Place or mechanizations, iPhone clients may now swipe between Lock Screens to draw in a comparing Concentration. Clients may likewise straightforwardly relate an Apple Watch face with a specific Concentration.

Center channels are one of the main upgrades to Centers in iOS 16. Center channels empower clients as far as possible inside applications like as Schedule, Mail, Messages, and Safari to show just pertinent material, for example, a specific Tab Gathering in Safari, an assortment of dates in the Schedule application, or email accounts in Mail. Designers might incorporate this capacity into their applications utilizing another Center channel Programming interface and change content in view of a client's ongoing Concentration.

Center mode design has likewise been upgraded, with a custom-made arrangement experience for every decision. Presently, iOS proposes a bunch of Home Screens and Lock Screens with matching applications, foundations, and gadgets for each Center mode. There are likewise extra adaptable settings inside Center modes, including the capacity to calm alarms from applications and people, subsequently offering the adaptability to discard warnings as opposed to only incorporate them, similar to the case in iOS 15.

ICLOUD SHARED PHOTOS LIBRARY

iCloud Shared Photo Library permits up to six family members to share pictures in a separate iCloud library. Users can share present images from their own collections, as properly as share relying on a begin date or persons in the photos. A new putting in the Camera app allows users to robotically share snap shots to the Shared Library. Additionally, customers will receive sensible hints to share a photo that consists of Shared Photo Library members.

Each client in the Common Photograph Library might add, eliminate, alter, or most loved the common photos or recordings, which show in their Recollections and Highlighted Photographs.

MESSAGES AND SHAREPLAY

Clients may now adjust or review as of late sent messages, recover as of late erased messages, and imprint conversations as uninitiated so they can get back to them later in iOS 16.

Moreover, SharePlay is coming to Messages, permitting you to appreciate synchronized content like motion pictures or tunes as well as shared playback controls while bantering in Messages.

With iOS 16, Apple refreshed the iMessage voice informing experience, making it its own independent iMessage application that stays in the application bar. Clients can tap, hold, and record messages all the more quickly with the application. The conventional hold and swipe-up signal to record voice messages has been supplanted by another Transcription button. On a comparable point, iOS 16 clients may now look at sound messages.

Notice proposals in iMessage currently incorporate a contact picture in the Fast Tap bar while referring to a contact. This is particularly valuable in bunch conversations on the grounds that various people might have a similar first name.

Mail

Clients might prepare of time and drop conveyance of a message as long as ten seconds before it arrives at a beneficiary's inbox. Mail perceives when a client neglects to add a basic part of their message, like a connection. Remind Later permits clients to restore a message whenever and date, and Follow Up suggestions naturally remind clients to circle back to an email on the off chance that they have not gotten a reaction.

Mail likewise contains a major patch up to look, which currently utilizes state of the art techniques to give more pertinent, precise, and exhaustive outcomes. At the point when clients begin looking for messages, they see late messages, contacts, archives, and connections.

WALLET AND APPLE PAY

Apple Pay Later

Clients in the US can use Apple Pay Later to extend the expense of an Apple Pay buy more than six weeks in four equivalent portions with no interest or charges. Apple Pay Later is coordinated into the Wallet application, where clients might track and return their installments. Clients might pursue Apple Pay Some other time while utilizing Apple Pay or by means of the Wallet application. Apple Pay Later is accessible wherever Apple Pay is acknowledged on the

web or in-application, as long as the Mastercard
network is utilized.

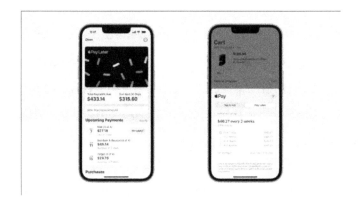

Apple Pay Request Following

Moreover, Apple Pay Request Following permits clients to get full receipts and request following data in Wallet for Apple Pay exchanges made with qualified dealers.

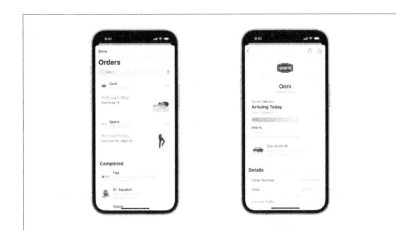

Computerized Keys and IDs

In iOS 16, support for keys and IDs in Wallet is broadened. Clients might involve their ID in Wallet to check their personality and age. For ideal insurance and protection, just the data expected for the exchange will be provided to the application, and the client can audit and authorization to share it utilizing Face ID or Contact ID. Moreover, clients may safely trade their home, inn, business, and car keys in Wallet through informing applications like Messages, Mail, and others.

Home

The iOS 16 Home app makes it easier for customers to explore, organize, and see their accessories, while improvements to the underlying architecture provide users with more efficient and reliable control over their smart home.

At the point when the Matter shrewd home network standard opens up later this harvest time, a later programming update to iOS 16 will incorporate similarity for it, permitting many accomplices to work flawlessly across stages.

Safari

In iOS 16, Safari has shared Tab Gatherings for imparting an assortment of sites to loved ones, simplifying it to add tabs and see how things are playing out.

Safari perusing is more secure with passkeys, which are remarkable computerized keys that are easy to involve and stay on the gadget for ideal insurance. Passkeys are intended to supplant passwords and utilize Contact ID or Face ID for biometric check, as well as iCloud Keychain to match up with start to finish encryption across iPhone, iPad, Macintosh, and Mac television. They will likewise work across applications and the web, and clients will actually want to utilize their iPhone to register to sites or applications on non-Apple gadgets.

Wellbeing AND Wellness

Wellbeing

The Wellbeing application presently incorporates Medications, which permits clients to handily make and keep a remedy list, set up timetables and updates, and screen their meds, nutrients, or enhancements. In the US, clients may basically point their iPhone camera at a name to add a medication, read about the drugs they're taking, and get a caution on the off chance that their solutions have conceivable huge collaborations.

Besides, clients may rapidly impart their Wellbeing information to friends and family and produce a PDF of accessible wellbeing records from connected wellbeing establishments promptly from the Wellbeing application.

Wellness

The Wellness application is currently open to all iPhone clients in iOS 16 to help screen and achieve wellness objectives, regardless of whether they own an Apple Watch. iPhone clients might utilize the Wellness application to lay out a day to day Move target and see how their dynamic calories assist with shutting the Move ring. Steps, distance, flights climbed, and exercises from outsider applications might be followed by iPhone movement sensors and transformed into a gauge of dynamic calories to add to clients' day to day Move objective. Clients can likewise persuade themselves by sharing their Move ring with others.

Maps

Apple Guides currently includes multistop steering; permitting clients to design up to 15 stops ahead of time and naturally sync courses from a Macintosh to an iPhone. Maps likewise gains travel refreshes, making it simple for riders to see how much their process will cost, add travel cards to Wallet, see low adjusts, and recharge travel cards, all without leaving the Guides application.

News

Apple News currently incorporates another My Games region where clients can essentially follow their number one groups and associations, get news from many top distributers, access scores, timetables, and standings for the best proficient and university associations, and view features straightforwardly in the News application.

LIVE TEXT AND VISUAL LOOK UP

Live Text can perceive text in both video and photographs. Clients might stop the film anytime and connect with the text. Clients may likewise right away change monetary forms, interpret text, and do different things with Live Text.

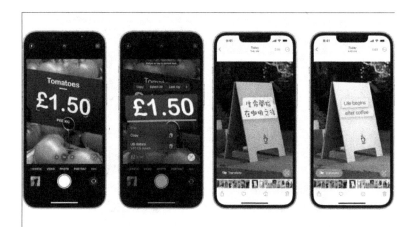

- Visual Gaze Upward develops photos with another element that permits clients to press and hang regarding the matter of a picture to lift it from the scenery and addition it in applications like Messages. Visual Look Into currently perceives birds, bugs, and landmarks.
- SIRI AND Correspondence

-

- In iOS 16, Siri can run alternate routes when an application is downloaded without requiring arrangement. Clients can undoubtedly add emoticon while communicating something specific, decide to send messages naturally, skirt the affirmation step, and hang up telephone and FaceTime calls sans hands by essentially saying "Hello Siri, hang up."

- Transcription gives an original encounter that permits clients to switch among discourse and contact effortlessly. Clients might utilize the console to type, tap in the text field, move the cursor, and info QuickType ideas without stopping Correspondence. Programmed accentuation and emoticon correspondence are currently accessible in Transcription.

-

- Different Highlights AND Enhancements

-

- · Customized Spatial Sound takes into account more precise tuning in. Audience members might use the TrueDepth camera on their iPhone to lay out a modified profile for Spatial

Sound, which gives a custom fitted listening experience.

-

- · Family Sharing makes it simple to set up a record for a kid with the fitting parental limitations set up immediately. It gives thoughts to progress in years fitting restrictions for applications, films, books, music, and different media, as well as an improved on system for setting up another gadget that naturally applies current parental controls. At the point when a young person demands extra screen time, guardians might acknowledge or decline the solicitation promptly in the Messages application.

- · Gaming Center has a redone dashboard that shows companions' down action and accomplishments in a single area, simplifying it for gamers to jump in and play with or go up against their companions.

-

- · Security Check is another protection include intended to help clients whose individual wellbeing is undermined by homegrown maltreatment by disavowing any entrance permitted to others quick. It contains a crisis reset highlight that permits clients to in a split second sign out of iCloud on the entirety of their different gadgets, reset security freedoms, and limit messages to the gadget in their grasp. It additionally helps clients in understanding and overseeing who and what applications they have conceded admittance to.

-

- · Openness refreshes incorporate Entryway Location, which permits clients who are visually impaired or have low vision to utilize their iPhone to explore the last couple of feet to their objective, and Apple Watch Reflecting, which permits clients with physical and engine inabilities to completely control Apple Watch from their iPhone utilizing assistive elements, for example, Voice Control and Switch Control. Besides, Live Inscriptions permit the Hard of hearing and Nearly deaf individuals to track with whether on a telephone or FaceTime call, using a videoconference or interpersonal interaction application, web based media material, or talking with somebody close to them.

-
- · Control Center's security history empowers clients to see which applications have as of late utilized their camera, amplifier, and area.

-
- · A patched up video player UI is more clear by eliminating pointless mess and underscoring central highlights like as volume, play/delay, and Picture in Picture.

-
- FaceTime currently has a clear call interface, as well as greater buttons for the camera, microphone, message, speaker, and SharePlay.
- Resolve difficulties with many contacts once and for all with a specialized option for highlighting and combining duplicate contacts.

- Use Bluetooth to transfer eSIM between iPhones when configuring cellular service in Settings.

- Settings have been improved, with a restructured iCloud settings page, an easier method to manage recognized Wi-Fi networks, and more.

- When connected to AirPods, a new appropriate glyph for your AirPods model will display in Control Center's Now Playing area and on the Lock Screen. This replaces the previous AirPlay icon, which remained static regardless of device.

- iOS 16 will now notify users if the system has stopped charging the iPhone due to overheating, which might shorten the battery's life. The new notice will appear on the Lock Screen, Notification Center, and the Settings Battery page.

- In iOS 16, Apple revamped the text and editing menu option, making it cleaner and now available in both bright and dark designs, depending on your iPhone's current mode. Apple has also changed the behavior of scrolling through choices in cases when the menu is lengthier.

- If you have unread messages from a specific contact, the Contacts widget will now notify you. The unread messages banner is only available on the Contacts app's medium and large-sized widgets.

IOS 16 SUPPORTED DEVICES

iOS 16 removed compatibility for several older devices that had previously been supported by iOS 13, iOS 14, and iOS 15, including the original iPhone SE, iPhone 6s and iPhone 6s Plus, iPhone 7 and iPhone 7 Plus, and the iPod touch. Since 2017, iOS 16 has been compatible with all iPhone models.

See the list of supported devices below:

- iPhone SE (2022)
- iPhone 13 Pro Max
- iPhone 13 Pro
- iPhone 13
- iPhone 13 mini
- iPhone 12 Pro Max
- iPhone 12 Pro
- iPhone 12
- iPhone 12 mini

- iPhone SE (2020)
- iPhone 11 Pro Max
- iPhone 11 Pro
- iPhone 11
- iPhone XS Max
- iPhone XS
- iPhone XR
- iPhone X
- iPhone 8 Plus
- iPhone 8

iOS 16: HOW TO CREATE A NEW IPHONE LOCK SCREEN

Apple has included numerous choices to customize the iPhone Lock Screen in iOS 16, which is presently in beta, including the capacity to modify the text style and variety, apply channels, and even add data rich gadgets to your experience.

You might pick from a scope of customisable Lock Screen backdrop styles, including moving pictures, Emoticon backgrounds, Apple Assortments and Tones, and dynamic Climate and Cosmology boards that reflect constant information.

With the expansion of Lock Screen gadgets, you might show data like as the climate, time, date, battery level, schedule occasions, cautions, time regions, Movement ring progress, and that's just the beginning, with Apple giving a gadget Programming interface to engineers.

You might make an exhibition of Lock Screen foundations and switch between them with a swipe. Assuming that you own an Apple Watch, you'll perceive the Lock Screen exhibition interface since it's very like the way in which watch face personalization works.

We should begin by making another Lock Screen utilizing the methods underneath.

1.Use Face ID or Contact ID to open your iPhone.

2.Tap and hold the Lock Screen.

3.Hit the blue + symbol, or swipe left until you arrive at the end, and afterward tap Add New.

4.Choose another backdrop starting from the drop menu, which incorporates Individuals, Photographs, Photograph Mix, Emoticon, Climate, Stargazing, Assortments, and Variety.

5. Change the plan of the clock and add gadgets above and underneath the time by tapping the edges at the highest point of the screen. Utilize the channel and picture decisions at the lower part of the screen to additionally customize it, which will modify in view of the kind of backdrop you've picked.

6. At the point when you're finished making your new Lock Screen, contact Done in the upper right corner, then, at that point, tap the screen again to leave the Lock Screen exhibition.

1. You might change the ongoing Lock Screen at any second by lengthy squeezing it and choosing the display view, or by going to Settings - > Backdrop and Lock Screens.

2. iOS 16: HOW TO Redo THE LOCK SCREEN

3.

4. With iOS 16, Apple totally updated the iOS Lock Screen, making it more configurable than any other time in recent memory and equipped

for showing data rich gadgets. This book will show you how to tweak your iPhone's Lock Screen with iOS 16, which is still being developed.

5.

6. You might customize the Lock Screen in iOS 16 with various text styles, colors, and, interestingly, gadgets. To start, simply open your iPhone utilizing Face ID or Contact ID, and afterward lengthy push on the Lock Screen to see the Lock Screen exhibition.

7.

8. The Lock Screen Display

9. Assuming you own an Apple Watch, you'll perceive the point of interaction since it's incredibly like the way that watch face personalization works. Lock Screens are partitioned into three classifications: Assortments (standard Apple Lock Screens), Photographs, and Varieties. Swipe left and right to choose a current Lock Screen, then lengthy press one to set it.

10. On the other hand, you might modify the presently chosen Lock Screen by tapping Redo,

or you can make another one by tapping the blue In addition to fasten. We'll focus on modifying a current Lock Screen in this part.

11.

12. Redoing Your Lock Screen

13. On the other hand, you might redo the as of now chosen Lock Screen by tapping Modify, or you can make another one by tapping the blue In addition to fasten. We'll focus on adjusting a current Lock Screen in this segment.

14. In the event that you're not kidding "Photograph" Lock Screen, the base decisions permit you to pick another image (or a choice of photos assuming it's a Mix backdrop), apply a channel, and enact or handicap the Viewpoint Zoom/Profundity Impact.

15. It's significant that the channels accessible by swiping left and right are brilliantly created consequently for the chose picture, so you'll get different conceivable outcomes relying upon whether it's a profundity photograph or a Variety backdrop. (Assuming it's a photograph, remember that utilizing various channels might bring about various typography styles being

applied to the time and date.) The settings at the lower part of the screen are more restricted in the event that you're planning a Lock Screen from Apple's "Assortments."

16.

17. There are outlines around the time and date at the top, as well as a hole beneath the time. The center edge shows that you might press to change the clock style, while the casings above and underneath it recommend that you can tap to add additional gadgets.

18. You might add gadgets over an opportunity to show some other time region, a predetermined caution, the following schedule occasion, a weather pattern, your action rings, the following update, and a chose stock. Gadgets that might be set underneath the time show additional data, for example, gadget battery levels, Schedule, Clock, Wellness, Home, News, Updates, Stocks, and Climate.

19. At the point when you're through planning your Lock Screen, press Done and afterward the screen again to leave the Lock Screen display. It's likewise significant that you might

change the ongoing Lock Screen by exploring to Settings - > Backdrop and Lock Screens.

20.

21. iOS 16: HOW TO Change TO An Alternate IPHONE LOCK SCREEN

22.

23. Apple has rolled out a few huge improvements to its versatile working framework in iOS 16, which is as of now in beta, including a total update of the Lock Screen.

24. On an iPhone running iOS 16, you can customize the Lock Screen in manners that weren't before possible, because of extra decisions for applying redid text styles, varieties, channels, and, interestingly, gadgets.

25. Perceiving that clients might need to make different Lock Screens to pick between, Apple has added a Lock Screen backdrop display that will seem natural to anyone who claims an Apple Watch, since it is very like the way in which watch face personalization works.

26. The backdrop display allows you to change your iPhone's Lock Screen in a hurry, while never leaving the Home Screen.

27. The directions underneath exhibit how to achieve this.

28.

29. 1.Use Face ID or Contact ID to open your iPhone.

30.　　　　Tap and hold the Lock Screen.

31. Swipe left or right in the gallery view to preview your Lock Screen backgrounds.

32. Simply touch on the wallpaper you want to use and it will be set as your active Lock Screen right away.

Is your backdrop display looking a piece exposed? Luckily, Apple has constructed various configurable Lock Screen backdrop sorts that you can add to your assortment, like moving photos, Emoticon settings, Apple Assortments and Varieties, and dynamic Climate and Cosmology shows that reflect continuous information.

IOS 16: HOW TO Rearrange BETWEEN Photographs ON YOUR IPHONE'S LOCK SCREEN

Apple has made huge upgrades to its versatile working framework in iOS 16, which is as of now in testing, including a full improving of the Lock Screen interface.

On an iPhone running iOS 16, you can customize the Lock Screen in manners that weren't before possible, because of extra decisions for applying modified textual styles, varieties, channels, and, interestingly, gadgets.

The choice to rearrange your Lock Screen foundation is one new element that is destined to be famous. You might pick different pictures from your photograph library and utilize the Blend choice to have the backdrop mix between them on a predefined hourly or everyday timetable, or at whatever point you wake or tap your iPhone screen.

The directions underneath will show you how to achieve it.

1.Turn on your iPhone and open it with Face ID or Contact ID.

2.Hold down the Lock Screen button until the backdrop display shows.

3.In the base right corner of the screen, tap the blue In addition to fasten.

4.From the backdrop choice, pick Photograph Mix.

5.Select a photos from your photograph library to rearrange, then press Add.

6.In the base right corner of the screen, tap the ellipsis button (the three ringed spots).

7.Select Everyday, Hourly, On Wake, or On Tap from the Mix Recurrence menu.

1.When got done, press Done in the upper right corner, then, at that point, tap your new Photograph Mix backdrop to pick it from the assortment.

IOS 16: HOW TO Do YOUR IPHONE SWITCH LOCK SCREENS In light of TIME OR Area

In iOS 16, Apple made various upgrades to Concentrate modes, one of which is the capacity to relate a custom Lock Screen with a specific Center mode. With the huge number of customisation decisions now accessible for Lock Screens, you might fit them to all the more likely suit your needs.

One of the decent highlights of iOS 16 is the capacity to redo Lock Screens to be more useful or commonsense, and afterward change to your particularly favored one as needs be. At the point when you're working, for instance, you might have a Lock Screen with work related gadgets and a family representation. At night, while you're settling down before bed, a fundamental Lock Screen with less gadgets and a loosening up dusk foundation can be ideal.

The lovely thing about joining a Lock Screen to a Center mode is that you can have the changeover to your customized Lock Screen happen consequently at a foreordained time or area. As found in the picture above, you might connect Lock Screens to existing Center modes by stirring things up around town button that shows up in the Lock Screen display, which is gotten to by lengthy squeezing your iPhone's as of now dynamic Lock Screen.

You may likewise pick a Lock Screen while laying out another Center mode in Settings.

This is the closely guarded secret in iOS 16, which is by and by in testing and will be accessible in the harvest time.

Making a Booked Concentration With a Custom Lock Screen

In this model, we've proactively planned a Lock Screen that we need to enact after the typical working day is finished, and we will connect it to a Center mode by adhering to the directions underneath.

1.On iPhone, explore to Settings - > Concentration and press the In addition to image in the upper right corner of the screen to add another Concentration.

2.On the following page, tap Custom, then, at that point, give your Center a name and a related symbol prior to tapping Straightaway.

3.Enable any warning quiet choices for people and applications when your Center is dynamic, then select the Lock Screen choice under "Alter Screens."

4.Select a current lock screen or make another one from the exhibition.

5.After you've connected your Lock Screen, hit Add Robotization under "Turn on naturally."

6.Select Time on the New Robotization screen.

7.Click Timetable and select the time and days of the week when you maintain that your Center should become dynamic.

Your new Center mode will this present time be enacted at a similar opportunity as your connected Lock Screen.

iOS 16 is currently in beta testing to empower Apple time to fix any blemishes and permit engineers to make their applications. A public delivery is made arrangements for the fall, probably around October.

www.ingramcontent.com/pod-product-compliance
Lightning Source LLC
LaVergne TN
LVHW051623050326
832903LV00033B/4628